T0268339

"As a longtime fan of Yumiko and a loyal customer of Fog Linen Work, I am thrilled for this book. These pages synthesize the minimal, beautiful, and gentle philosophy that drew me to her work to begin with. At a time when the world feels chaotic, Yumiko's Japanese rituals and ideas bring calmness and purpose."

—Aran Goyoaga, author of *Cannelle et Vanille*

"Yumiko has been a part of my home for the better part of a decade—and it's more than just her Fog Linen Work towels, aprons, and napkins. It's her sensibility, captured beautifully in this book. *Simplicity at Home* embodies the idea that a pared down life of intention leaves space for all sorts of moments, magic, and rituals to be explored."

—Heidi Swanson, author of *Super Natural Cooking*

"As a fellow shop owner and designer of objects, I thoroughly enjoy delving into the broader community of like-minded creatives, and I have long been a fan of Yumiko's work. This book celebrates our shared values of simplicity and thoughtful design in the home, which have been beautifully captured within these pages."

—Sibella Court, owner of The Society inc and author of *Etcetera: Creating Beautiful Interiors with the Things You Love* and *Imaginarium: A Compendium of Inspiration*

Simplicity at Home

Japanese Rituals,
Recipes, and Arrangements
for Thoughtful Living

Simplicity at Home

Yumiko Sekine, Founder of Fog Linen Work
with Jenny Wapner

Photography by Nao Shimizu

CHRONICLE BOOKS
SAN FRANCISCO

I dedicate this book to my family—Goban and Wataru.

And to a few of the people who have inspired me with their beautiful work:
Sally and Mark Bailey, Lotta Jansdotter, Erica Tanov, Tricia Foley, and Sibella Court.

Library of Congress Cataloging-in-Publication Data available.

ISBN: 978-1-7972-0295-2

Manufactured in China.

Design by Vanessa Dina.
Typesetting by Howie Severson.
Photographs by Nao Shimizu.

10 9 8 7 6 5 4

Chronicle books and gifts are available at special quantity
discounts to corporations, professional associations, literacy
programs, and other organizations. For details and discount
information, please contact our premiums department at
corporatesales@chroniclebooks.com or at 1-800-759-0190.

Chronicle Books LLC
680 Second Street
San Francisco, California 94107
www.chroniclebooks.com

CONTENTS

My Life
with Linen

Several years ago, my friend Stephanie came to Tokyo from New York and stayed at our house for a few days. After her visit, she told me how different my life was from what she expected. When I asked her what she thought life would be like here in Japan, she said she pictured busy crosswalks crowded with people, noisy streets with huge billboards, and people living in small, cramped apartments packed full of stuff. Instead, what she found was a calm house, with just a few things, where life was simple and relaxed. I think many people share Stephanie's expectations about Japanese life. Even though Japan has become such a popular tourist destination, I suspect there are still a lot of foreigners who don't know how Japanese people really live.

My lifestyle and aesthetic—simple, minimal, a mix of Japanese and Western influences—is common here, but it may not be familiar to people outside of the country. *Simplicity at Home* is my chance to show you this modern Japanese style, and how you can adapt it to suit your own home and life.

As I write this, I've just finished moving into a new house, one that my boyfriend, Wataru Ohashi, and I built ourselves. I've spent a lot of time thinking about the best way to inhabit this new space, which has given me fresh eyes and a renewed desire to live richly with less, and to find more simplicity and ease in my life. I hope these lessons will be of value to you, and that in simplifying your home, you will find more clarity and joy in your life.

The combination of Japanese and Western influences in my life reflects my family history. I grew up in Morioka, a city in northern Japan known

for its traditional crafts. My family ran a hospital there, and my maternal grandmother was one of its doctors, an unusual profession for a woman of her generation. In addition to seeing patients and running the hospital, she volunteered with the widows of World War II veterans. She created a workshop where they could make and sell scarves, hats, other clothing, and blankets. This workshop, called Michinoku Akane Kai, is still active today. The shop buys fleece so the women can spin and dye the yarn themselves, and then use that yarn for weaving and knitting. I've worn their products since I was little and still use some of them now, forty years later. I even carry their products in my stores.

My grandmother traveled all over the world as a UNESCO ambassador and hosted foreign students and guests at her house. These visitors made a big impression on my mother, who developed a fascination with Western Europe and the United States. She loved the clothes, knickknacks, and food these visitors brought as gifts. As an adult, she emulated a Western style of decorating, and my childhood home had many decidedly un-Japanese features: wooden floors, a brick-walled kitchen, a fireplace, silver utensils, and Royal Copenhagen dishes. My mother carried on the family tradition of cultural exchange by hosting foreign visitors in our home throughout my childhood.

While my mother's family was strongly influenced by Western cultures, my paternal grandmother celebrated our homegrown customs. One of her greatest passions was teaching the formal Japanese tea ceremony. She had a dedicated room for it in her house and gave lessons to adults and children in our community. I took a few lessons when I was in high school, but sadly, I was not patient enough to learn this beautiful Japanese custom. I had my eyes on the West.

When I moved to Tokyo for college, I got a part-time job at a small gift shop and café that resembled an English country cottage. One day, the owner pulled me aside to show me books by the American entertaining pioneer Lee Bailey. We cooked recipes from his books to serve in the café, and sold dishes and linens in the gift shop similar to those pictured in his books. I loved those books and still have a copy of *Lee Bailey's Country Weekends* (1983) in my kitchen.

When I was in my early twenties, I got a job working for a small bookstore that sold foreign books, mostly about decorating and cooking. It was my dream job—reading through the books and writing short book descriptions in Japanese. I spent my days immersed in books by Martha Stewart, Tricia Foley, and the British designers Tricia Guild and Terence Conran.

The bookstore was run by a group of successful businessmen who started the store as a passion project. Nevertheless, they could not ignore the fact that it was losing money. Without an improvement in sales, I would lose my job. I suggested that instead of selling new books, we could attract a more targeted audience by selling a carefully curated selection of used and rare books from around the world. The

owners liked the idea but wouldn't pay me to travel abroad to find the books to sell. Instead, they offered me paid time off to take the trip and the promise that I could keep the profits from any sales.

After spending all of my savings on my first trip to New York, I came back with decorating and food magazines, children's books, and lots of cookbooks. I still remember a few of the titles from that that first trip: *Betty Crocker's Picture Cook Book* (1998), *Miss B.'s First Cookbook*, by Peggy Hoffman (1950), and the Peter Pauper Press set of vintage cookbooks. I bought books that appealed to me personally and ones that I knew would seem special to customers in Tokyo. It only took me a week to sell through everything I had brought back. I made subsequent trips to Boston, Atlanta, San Francisco, Los Angeles, Portland, Santa Fe, Austin, Seattle, and Vancouver, and then on to Europe.

It was on a trip to San Francisco that I noticed some handcrafted wire baskets in the window of a housewares store next to my hotel. The shop was closed every time I walked by, but on my last day in the city, I happened to pass by just as the owner was going into the building. I stopped her and asked about the baskets. It turned out they were from Mexico, and she had an assortment of many different styles. I thought they would be popular in Japan and was pleased to learn that she could ship them in large quantities.

By then, I had left the bookstore and was working independently, selling books to gift shops around Tokyo. I thought those baskets could be my entry point to selling housewares, something I had been wanting to do. The process of buying and selling books had been fun and exciting but labor-intensive, requiring long hours of sorting through piles of them. While traveling, I made countless trips to post offices to ship boxes of books back to Japan. I was tired from all the travel and suspected that importing housewares might offer me a respite. The ordering could be done from home via fax. And down the road, I might even open my own shop.

Around this time, my great-aunt began traveling to Lithuania to spend time with a family she had become close with. Like her sister (my grandmother), my great-aunt had also hosted exchange students. A student from Lithuania had stayed with her while his country was struggling for independence from Russia in the early 1990s. Caught in this tumultuous historic moment and unable to return to his country, he was helped by my great-aunt, who got his family to Japan, where they could live and work until it was safe to return to their country. Once they returned to Lithuania, my great-aunt would visit them often. After several trips, she liked it so much, she decided to open a Japanese restaurant in Vilnius, the capital.

Intrigued by my great-aunt's love of Lithuania, I agreed to join her on one of her trips to the country. I was interested in linens and knew about Lithuania's reputation for high-quality textiles; I was excited to see them for myself. I expected to find shops filled with simple, beautifully made linen goods, but it was eight years after their war for independence and the shops were empty. Two days before I was scheduled to leave, and still without having made contact with any linen manufacturers, I looked in the phone book for *linas*, or "linen" in Lithuanian. Once I got back to Tokyo, I wrote to several of the companies listed and asked for samples. Only two of them responded. But instead of the expected catalogs and price lists, I received a few little scraps of linen. I would need to create a few of my own designs and ask for quotes and minimum orders to get started. Until then, I had not planned to do any of my own designs. But I actually had a pretty clear image in my mind of what I wanted, and the process of getting that image down on paper was surprisingly easy. I sent six sketches of design ideas with measurements: a kitchen towel, a tote bag, a napkin, and three styles of aprons. In a couple of weeks, I received the first samples. They turned out just as I had imagined! My first collection started just like that, with those six items. Many of these continue to be our bestsellers.

Six months after that first visit, I returned to Lithuania, this time with the intention of seeing the factory and meeting the workers. The factory owner was resistant, but I explained that my wholesale customers cared a lot about how the products were made. He took me back to the sewing room, where there were six or seven Lithuanians working. It reminded me of my sewing class in high school. The workers were all highly skilled, and the production was on a very small scale.

During that first year, communication with my supplier was difficult. He would suggest bright colors and lots of decorative elements, and I would remind him that I wanted everything to be as simple as possible. Then he came to Tokyo. I took him to the stores where the products were being sold, and he quickly learned how Japanese tastes differed. Now he is a true partner, suggesting new fabrics and helping to refine our product line.

My aesthetic reflects all of these influences: my grandmothers and mother, the café I worked in during college, and even the books I pored over in those early days. It's American and European culture and styles blended with Japanese traditions. I've been lucky to be exposed to so many ways of living, beginning at such a young age, and through Fog Linen I have encountered many more sources of inspiration.

I never stop collecting ideas from my everyday life. Often the process begins when I look for a product and discover that it doesn't exist. Or it does exist, but not in a way that I find appealing. For instance, I wanted a bath towel made of thick linen, one that absorbs water well but does not trap germs like thick terry cloth cotton towels do. I've also searched in vain for a small, simply designed oven mitt just big enough to cover and protect the hand, as well as linen bags without logos—one of the hardest things to find. These are products that I've designed and we now sell at Fog Linen.

I've been running Fog Linen for twenty years now and truthfully, it hasn't changed much in that time. I continue to stock the things I personally have used and love. There are just more of them, and I'm able to bring them to more and more people around the world. Our designs are basically the same, and I still sell those wire baskets I found in San Francisco so many years ago. Now, in addition to our linen products, we carry handcrafted housewares made in India.

My workday routine has also stayed pretty much the same over the years. I like to be the first one in the office. I tidy up and change the displays. I plan and lay out the seven catalogs we produce every year. I regularly talk with our customers, some of whom have been shopping with us for many years. All of this keeps me busy and connected with the people who share my love of linen.

Linen itself continues to be my greatest source of inspiration. When I see a bed made with simple linen sheets, dry off from a shower with a well-made linen towel, or sit down to dinner at a table set with a linen tablecloth, I'm reminded of how much I love this durable, timeless fabric. It's the thing I miss the most when I travel. Coming home, I remember how much I love the feel of linen, and how lucky I am to be surrounded by it in my life.

As my style continues to evolve, the biggest challenge has been to find ways to live comfortably with less. Wataru has been my biggest inspiration in this pursuit. An architect, he lives with very little; in fact, he could probably fit all of his belongings into a single suitcase. I don't think I could ever achieve that level of minimalism, but I have fewer things than I did before.

The process of creating a rich life and a beautiful home with less is the inspiration for this book. I call my approach "joyfully minimalist" because I believe that with less, you can find greater enjoyment in what you do have. In these pages, I share practical ideas for creating a less cluttered home, and ways to instill more pleasure and meaning in the time you spend there. I show you how to prepare your house for the changing seasons; how to create a small garden, even when you don't have much space; and how to repair and repurpose belongings that may be old or worn, but could be given a new life.

Repairing broken dishes, finding new uses for scraps of fabric, and dying stained clothes are examples of a kind of resourcefulness that not only saves money but also demonstrates the beauty in things that are slightly imperfect. Many of these ideas are inspired by Japanese traditions, but they work equally well in the West.

This book is also a personal record of my ongoing experiment with practical and thoughtful minimalism. I begin in the summer because that is when I moved into a new house and applied a more critical lens to my habits. The house was a clean slate and a welcome opportunity to be more deliberate about how I decorate, how I interact with my space, and really, how I live.

SUMMER

As a child, I loved many things about summer: the big fire-works festivals called *hanabi*; wearing *yukata*, or the thin kimono designed for warm weather; swimming in the nearby river; and attending the morning glory festival every July. I would spend the long days outside, returning home well past nightfall.

However, unlike in northern Japan where I grew up, summers in Tokyo are unbearably hot and getting even hotter. Now I escape the heat by staying inside and working on various projects and crafts. I'll venture outside in the evening, once the city has cooled down. This year, since we moved into a new house, I was glad to have long days to spend indoors mending things like broken ceramics and organizing drawers and shelves. In addition to moving furniture and unpacking, there were so many projects to be done! I recycled old bed sheets into curtains, started a rooftop garden, and aranged furniture.

When summer arrives, I change the textiles around my house as well as my wardrobe. I switch to lighter weight sheets and blankets, but use a darker color palette, which makes me feel cooler. I also change my eating habits in the summer months, switching to *mugicha*, a cold barley tea, and eating cold somen noodles. We make tempura with the vegetables from our garden and serve it alongside the noodles.

I love inviting friends over to share a simple and delicious late-summer meal like the one featured in this chapter. In the following pages, you'll find the recipe for this easy meal, as well as ideas for making your house lighter and cooler during the warmer months.

Creating a New Home
Reconsidering What You Really Need

When the construction of our new home was finally done, I walked around the empty house, loving the absence of things. I've always thought it is more luxurious to have space rather than many possessions. As much as I wished we could have kept the house as it was, we needed to move in by the end of the month. And so, we packed up everything up from the old house and it was delivered the next Saturday afternoon.

Before unpacking all the boxes, I sat in the new house and thought hard about what we absolutely needed for those first few days. The list was not long:

Towels, toothbrush, soap
Pajamas, underwear
Table and chairs
Glasses for water
Kettle and coffee maker
Dishes and cutlery
Kitchen towels
Bed and sheets

After spending a day with just the items above, I wondered what I even had in the dozens of unpacked boxes. Was it all necessary?

I have moved homes and offices twelve times in my life, and each time, it was a lot work. Moving makes me realize how many unused and unnecessary things I hold onto, and how nice it would be to live and work with less. So when my boyfriend Wataru and I were preparing to move this time, I considered each item carefully to determine whether I really needed it or not. Unsurprisingly, many things had to go.

I brought some to the recycling center, some I sold in front of my store, and some I had to pay to throw away. In Japan, there is a fairly steep fee to dispose of trash, which is a good system because it really makes you think about throwing things away—or buying them in the first place! Even after this long process, we still had thirty big, heavy boxes, plus furniture and clothing, which seemed like a lot for just the two of us.

Whether you're moving or not, it's good to periodically review your belongings to see if you really need everything you own. When is the last time you used it? Do you only use something for special occasions? Does it lie, forgotten, at the back of a drawer?

Starting to Fill the Shelves
Displaying Little Treasures

When we were planning our new house, I wanted to use as much of the square footage for living space as possible, which meant forfeiting big closets and other closed-off storage spaces and opting instead for open shelving. I like open shelving for a number of reasons: I often forget where I put things, and when everything is on display, it's easier to find what I'm looking for. It's also more inviting. I want visitors and houseguests to feel comfortable searching for the things they need without tentatively opening drawers. But most important, if an object is in our house, I want it to be something I won't mind looking at every day. Open shelving does require a little extra thought, and when I buy something, I immediately think about where I will put it. I also think about how to arrange and display things to avoid visual clutter. I spend so much time organizing and displaying merchandise in my stores that this process has become second nature to me, even at home. Here are a few of my tips for organizing shelves:

right: These are our living room shelves. We keep photography books, other large books, and magazines on the bottom shelves. I always try to leave the top three shelves open to display artwork. Every few months I'll check each book to see if I still like reading it or if it has useful information. If not, it's time to say goodbye. And when I get a new book, I try to find one I can remove to keep the shelf balanced and uncrowded.

- When you arrange items on a shelf, it's important to leave space between objects. People tend to fill up the entire space, but it will create a more tranquil and less cluttered look if you take a few things out. This same principle applies to the arrangement of objects on dressers, tables, and mantels.

- Group items by color or size. For example, I have a shelf for clear glasses and another for white dishes. When arranging books, once I've organized them by genre, I try to group them by height.

- Use boxes or baskets for storing small items, and be sure to store similar items together.

- To keep your space organized, it is important to designate a spot for every item and return it to its proper place after using it.

- Being forced to look at your possessions makes you think about them differently. If you only have cabinets with doors, try removing the doors and see if that changes the way you organize and use your belongings. I bet it will encourage you to be a bit more deliberate in how you use that space.

Blue Skies

A voyage across 16 blue skies, selected by their collector, for issue 40 of Un Sedicesimo

1. Morocco 2. Portugal
3. The Netherlands
4. Thailand 5. New Zealand
6. Japan 7. Norway
8. Germany 9. France
10. Hungary 11. Russia
12. Spain 13. Kazakhstan
14. USA 15. Britain 16. Italy

SHOPPING INSOLITE à PARIS

OPEN STUDIOS with Lotta Jansdotter

MEOW!

NAKSAI DAVID

MENU

Alexander Calder

Antonio Lopez

Reflections From Asia

bill

IMPERFECT HOME

B.L.T. ■ NEW

美術の歴史

三島由紀夫の家

simple

TIR

left: These shelves are made from old repurposed scaffolding. I have grouped similar items together, teas and spices on the top right shelf and glass flower vases on the lower one. We use wine boxes to store tablecloths.

above: Galvanized steel boxes help me organize silverware. Chopsticks in one box, serving spoons in another, etc. When we have guests over, we can just take the box from the drawer directly to the table.

left: I organize shelves by color and type, making sure to allow for space between items.

above: I keep all Japanese and other Asian dishes in one drawer. Right now, they all fit perfectly, but when I buy a new dish, I'll likely let one go to make space for it.

left: Organizing small things in the bathroom is challenging. I opted for a cabinet with a door, but I still try to corral things into small glass jars for a less cluttered look. And I always look for ways to make everyday objects more pleasant to look at.

Summer Bed Linens

A Cooler Palette and Lighter Fabrics for Hot Nights

In the summer, linen cools me down, and in the winter, it covers my body softly and warms me up. It is miraculous that way. Linen's fibers make it very absorbent, so you don't wake up overheated and sweaty.

Every night when I get into bed, I feel so lucky to be in this business, surrounded by linen. I know linen bedding may seem expensive, but consider the amount of time you spend in your bed. A linen sheet is a little more than the price of a nice shirt. You don't wear the same shirt every day, but you can sleep on the same sheets every night.

At Fog Linen, we sell mostly neutral-colored bed linens. I love the look of an all-white bed; it's like a blank slate, and helps me settle my mind and calm my body. Natural-colored linens are special too, because they haven't been bleached or dyed. They feel untouched; you can almost smell the earth on the fiber. But last summer we had a terrible heat wave, and I was searching for relief. I thought darker colors might create a sense of cool, so I added a few darker shades to our collection.

In this effort to cool down the bedroom, I also played around with different arrangements for my bed. I found that on the hot summer nights, it helped to put the mattress directly on the floor, since heat rises. This is more traditional in Japan than raising a mattress on a bed frame. These small changes did help, and it was a nice reminder that little adjustments can have a big impact on comfort.

above top: **This is our unbleached, natural linen. I love its smell, which reminds me of straw drying in the sun.**

above bottom: **Although it's a very simple fold-out bed, when it's made up with freshly washed and ironed white sheets, it ends up feeling very special.**

above: One of the easiest ways to make a space feel uncluttered is to limit the color palette to neutrals.

above: I opted for the very simple and streamlined look of two matching oak bed frames pushed together to create a double bed. I believe a very pared down bedroom like this is best for sleep.

Recycling Old Linen Sheets

A New Life for Favorite Textiles

I bought my first set of linen sheets when I was about twenty-five years old. I had just started a wholesale business and was barely scraping by. I read an essay by a Japanese writer living in Italy. She wrote about watching her neighbor wash his linen sheets every morning in order to have freshly laundered linen sheets to sleep on every night. I thought that sounded like the most luxurious life and wanted to try it myself.

I found Irish linen sheets in a boutique in Tokyo. They were very expensive, more than I had ever spent on sheets, and I could barely afford them, but I rationalized the purchase by thinking that if I used them every day for the next five years, it would be worth it. And they would make me so happy. Like the Italian man in the essay, I washed my sheets every morning and slept on freshly laundered linen every night. And not only did it make me very happy; I also kept those sheets for much longer than five years.

Now, twenty-five years later, the sheets have a few stains and some holes. I still have them, but I've repurposed the fabric. I used some of the linen to make curtains, and the rest I cut into strips so my talented assistant Chihiro could transform them into useful household objects, in this case, by weaving the strips of fabric into hot pads and a table runner. There are endless uses for beautiful fabric that has outlived its intended use. It gives me such pleasure to find a new life for a beloved object.

above top: Hot pad woven from a linen sheet. The linen thread and white fabric match perfectly.

above bottom: Place mat woven from a linen sheet with a small Clover handloom. Once you set the thread and fabric tape, you can make a place mat like the one shown in a few hours.

above: A Clover handloom for small home weaving projects. (It can be ordered online.)

Setting the Table with Handmade Ceramics

Making an Ordinary Meal Feel Special

I try to live with less, but I have a weakness for dishes. Especially when I travel, it's hard to resist beautiful and unusual ceramics. In addition to admiring them as objects, I love that interesting dishes on a table can make my simple and somewhat ordinary food feel special and worthy of celebrating. Japan has so many ceramicists that make beautiful handmade pottery with unique shapes, as well as handblown glassware. They are often specific to the style of a particular region, but they can be easily mixed and matched with other pieces.

One of the big changes I've noticed in Japan is that contemporary ceramics are used with Western food as well as Japanese. When I was young, it was uncommon for Japanese families to cook European, American, or even other Asian foods at home. But now, with so many cooking shows and magazines featuring these cuisines, and with a more diverse population in Japan, ceramic designers have adapted as well.

Ironically, I learned how to use Japanese dishes from my foreign friends. When I moved to Tokyo for college, I lived alone in a small apartment. I cooked mostly Western food at home, and I served it on Western-style dishes, so I wasn't particularly interested in Japanese ceramics. When my friends from the United States and Europe visited me in Tokyo, they would ask me to help them find nice Japanese dishes. And when I visited them in their homes, I saw how beautiful Western food looked on Japanese dishes. Now I incorporate Japanese ceramics into all my table settings, regardless of what I'm serving.

Kozara, which are small dishes, make nice accents on the table when filled with spices or dips. Larger bowls, called *fukazara*, intended for ramen or udon, can be used as serving bowls. A *katakuch*, or spouted pourer, is great for sauces or dressings. While I collect different styles of dishes, I do try to limit their colors so the table doesn't feel too busy. I stick with white, gray, black, and sometimes indigo blue. These colors don't overshadow or compete with the colors of the food or the table linens.

In Tokyo, my favorite ceramics store is Zakka. They have a thoughtfully selected collection of simple pottery. Every piece they sell is beautifully made but still practical enough to use

every day. I also love the gift shop at the Japan Folk Crafts Museum, which sells traditional housewares from all over the country. Most of their collection is reasonably priced, and it's a good cross-section of simple, authentic pottery. When you look at the ceramics on display at the museum, you understand how Japanese pottery has been influenced by that of neighboring China and Korea.

And, of course, the antique market in Tokyo is always a fun place to shop. There is a mix of Japanese and non-Japanese things; some are very old, and some are not old at all. If I find something I like, it feels like a once-in-a-lifetime opportunity because the same vendor might not be there next week and I would never find that same dish at a store. It's hard to pass that up.

48
|
49

below: Bamboo colanders are really useful for cooking. I find them so pleasing to look at that I serve food in them as well. They come in a variety of different shapes and sizes and are perfect for holding noodles or cut vegetables.

left: Sori Yanagi cutlery. The black wooden handle looks dramatic and fits comfortably in the hand. They also make pots and pans and porcelain dinner-ware. I love the look of black cutlery on the table.

left: Simple Japanese dishes for every-day use, each one slightly different. I collect them in neutral colors like beige, gray, white, and black.

left: I set out kozara (small dishes) to hold dipping sauces and garnishes like chopped herbs, bonito flakes, sesame seeds, dried seaweed, grated daikon, grated ginger, and miso. You can also use kozara as prep bowls while you are cooking.

above top: Uniquely shaped handblown glasses in different sizes are good for water, juice, milk, beer, and wine.
Many of the ones shown here are made by the same
glass artist, Naomi Shioya.

above bottom: Handmade ceramic bowls for eating rice,
soup, salad, or noodles. These are our everyday dishes,
which I use for Japanese food, as well as Western food and
other types of Asian food.

above top: Little sake cups and server. At restaurants in Japan, diners often get to pick the sake cups they will drink from. It's always fun to pick your favorite and see which ones your friends pick.

above bottom: Large serving bowls, which I use for soup, pasta, and salad.

above: While I rarely buy patterned dishes, opting instead for single colors, I treasure these hand-painted dishes by California artist Sherry Olsen.

Cold Noodles with Two Types of Tempura

An Easy Summer Meal

SERVES 4

In Japan, we relish the small signs of a new season's arrival and mark the passing of the previous one. This deep appreciation of the rhythms of nature is clearly expressed in our cuisine. Food that is in season is called "shun," and it is one of the most important factors in deciding what to eat.

During the hot and humid days of summer, I lose my appetite for most foods. The exception is tempura and somen. Tempura, batter-fried vegetables and seafood, is almost universally loved. It can be made year-round, but in the summer, you can take advantage of all the beautiful vegetables that are in season. *Kakiage* is a type of tempura made with a combination of vegetables or seafood, or both. Sometimes larger vegetables are cut into matchsticks to be battered and fried together. Tempura, by contrast, is made with individual pieces of vegetables or seafood.

Somen are very thin noodles made from wheat flour and dried. They are popular in the summer, since they are served cold and are satisfying without being heavy. You can buy them in the Asian section of well-stocked grocery stores. They are very quickly boiled, then transferred to a bamboo colander. To eat them, you first dip each bite in a sauce made from dashi and soy sauce.

For this simple meal, I use a variety of summer vegetables at peak ripeness—kabocha squash, edamame, okra, and corn—which I have either grown in my container garden or found at the local market. This meal is particularly delicious served with cold beer or chilled barley tea.

Okra and Kabocha Tempura

8 oz [225 g] kabocha squash
Small handful of okra (about 8 pods)
1½ cups [360 ml] vegetable oil
½ cup [120 ml] cold sparkling water
¼ cup [30 g] cake flour
Kosher salt

Cut the kabocha in half, from stem to root, and scoop out the seeds.
Cut into thin slices. Trim both ends of the okra.

In a large, heavy-bottomed pan over medium heat, heat the oil to 350°F
[180°C].

Combine the sparkling water and cake flour in a medium bowl. Add the
vegetables and coat well.

Add two or three vegetables at a time to the hot oil, being careful not
to crowd the pan. Fry, undisturbed, for 3 to 4 minutes until lightly golden
and crispy. Remove with a slotted spoon and drain on a paper towel–
lined plate. Salt immediately. Repeat until all of the vegetables have
been cooked. You can reserve the oil for making the Corn and Edamame
Kakiage (recipe follows).

Somen

2 Tbsp soy sauce
2 Tbsp mirin (sweet cooking wine)
1 tsp sugar
½ cup [6 g] bonito flakes
Two 9½ oz [270 g] packages dried somen noodles

To make the dipping sauce, combine the soy sauce, mirin, sugar, and ½ cup plus 2 Tbsp [150 ml] of water in a small saucepan. Bring to a boil, remove from the heat, and add the bonito flakes. Let sit for 5 minutes. Strain the sauce through a fine-mesh strainer into a bowl or measuring cup and refrigerate for at least 30 minutes. The bonito flakes can be discarded.

Bring a large pot of water to a boil and add the noodles and another 1 cup [240 ml] of water. Return to a boil, lower the heat, and simmer the noodles until just tender and slightly translucent, about 2 minutes. Drain the noodles in a colander and rinse well under cold running water.

To serve, transfer the somen to a large bamboo basket. Pour the dipping sauce into four small bowls. Dip each bite of noodles into the sauce before eating.

Corn and Edamame Kakiage (Mixed Vegetable Tempura)

1 ear corn, husked
Kosher salt
1 cup [200 g] fresh (preferable) or frozen edamame, in their shells
1½ cups [360 ml] vegetable oil
⅓ cup [40 g] cake flour
⅓ cup [75 ml] cold sparkling water

Cut the kernels off the corn cob and set aside, discarding the cob.

Fill a medium saucepan with lightly salted water, bring to a boil, and cook the edamame for 3 minutes. Drain and shell the edamame.

In a large, heavy-bottomed pan over medium heat, heat the oil to 350°F [180°C]. Line a plate with paper towels.

Meanwhile, combine the cake flour and sparkling water in a medium bowl. Add the corn and edamame and coat well, or coat them separately.

Using a flat ladle or slotted spoon, scoop up a spoonful of the coated vegetables and gently release them into the hot oil, using the side of the pan as a guide so they don't tumble into the oil and fall apart. The cluster of vegetables should be about 3 in [7.5 cm] wide. Let the vegetables fry, undisturbed, for 3 to 4 minutes until the batter is lightly golden and crispy. Remove with a slotted spoon and drain on the paper towel–lined plate. Salt immediately. Repeat until all of the corn and edamame have been cooked.

above: A popular summer sweet called *anmitsu*. This traditional dessert is made with boiled adzuki beans, cubes of agar gelatin, sweet rice flour dumplings, dried plums, sweet bean paste, and brown sugar syrup.

above top: Drying the bamboo colanders after cooking. Bamboo colanders are made all over Japan. Each region makes a slightly different style, and it's fun to seek out different weaves and shapes to create a unique and diverse collection.

above bottom: An informal happy hour spread with cold beer and fried fava beans, called *soramame.*

The Art of Kintsugi

How to Mend Broken Ceramics and Embrace the Beauty of Imperfection

It is always sad when you break a favorite ceramic bowl or glass—especially when it's a family heirloom, a favorite find from a craft market, or a piece discovered on a special adventure. Many of them carry fond memories of past meals and travels. But as Buddha said, "All worldly things are impermanent." Whenever a dish was broken in my childhood home, often by me or my sister, my mother always repeated the Buddha's words.

My mother collects dishes, coordinating them with her table linens to make each meal look festive. And though she must have been sad to see the dishes broken, she would gather the pieces and give them a new life with *kintsugi*. With this traditional method of repairing ceramics, the broken pieces are joined with urushi lacquer, which is painted with a gold powder paste after it dries. Kintsugi is more than a way to mend a broken dish; it transforms the dish into a piece of art. With the gold line marking the repaired seam, each dish is unique. Kintsugi is a perfect expression of the Japanese concept of *wabi-sabi*, which is about finding beauty in imperfection, particularly the inevitable process of age and decay.

In our respective homes, my parents and I have many dishes with this telltale gold line. I love sharing this technique with others, since it's relatively simple to do and saves broken dishes from the trash bin. I encourage you to gather up your broken treasures and try kintsugi for yourself.

The supplies can be purchased at art supply stores or from online retailers. It's a good idea to wear gloves and make sure your work space is well ventilated. The finished dish is food safe.

MATERIALS

Urushi lacquer

Small paintbrush

Dry cloth

800-grit sandpaper

Gold or mica powder

Clear epoxy resin

Paper or cardboard

High-quality, fine-point detail paintbrush

Agate burnisher

1. Make sure your ceramic pieces are clean and dry.

2. Carefully apply the urushi lacquer to one of the broken edges using a small paintbrush.

3. Align this piece with its matching piece and press them together. Repeat with any remaining pieces.

4. Remove any excess lacquer with a dry cloth, then let the lacquer dry for at least 6 hours or overnight.

5. Once dry, lightly sand any lacquer that has seeped onto the surface.

6. Prepare the gold or mica paste by mixing equal parts powder and epoxy resin on a sheet of paper or cardboard. (This dries quickly, so don't mix it until you are ready to use it.) With the fine brush, apply a small amount of gold powder paste along the broken line. Allow it to dry for about 10 hours or overnight.

7. Lightly polish the gold line with the agate burnisher.

AUTUMN

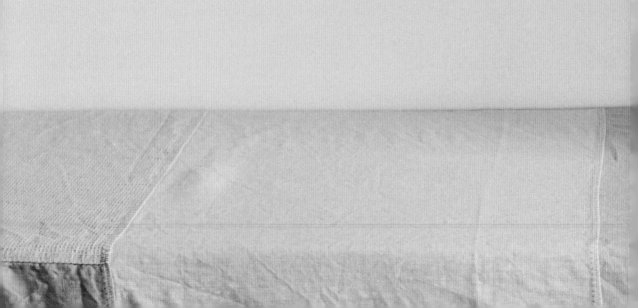

Autumn is my favorite time of the year. The weather is mild, and trees across the city glow yellow, orange, and red. I spend my weekends outside as much as possible, taking long walks around the city. I'll stroll down the narrow streets, visiting boutiques, cafés, and bookshops, and even after decades of living in Tokyo, I always discover something new.

These days, I often end up at the farmers market, which has become one of my favorite destinations. The market yields a true autumn bounty: chestnuts, persimmons, new harvest rice, and mushrooms. Growers and food artisans from all over the region come to the market to sell their fruits, vegetables, and food products. I love discovering new varietals, and the vendors are always generous with their time, sharing ideas for new recipes and tips for making the most of fall foods.

This year, I was inspired to start a garden filled with flowering trees and shrubs to attract birds and butterflies, with places to sit and relax. Over the summer, I had planted herbs and vegetables in raised beds in our rooftop garden, and in the autumn, I harvested the remains of the summer crop, drying tomatoes and herbs to enjoy throughout the autumn and into the winter.

After spending the summer in sleeveless tops and dresses, I welcome the opportunity to think about fall fashions, incorporating heavier fabrics into my wardrobe and layering pieces for more texture and warmth. I pack away and store my lighter clothes until the next year and pull out my long-sleeved tops and dresses. I love seeing the spectrum of fall colors reflected in my closet. I go through this same process for my house, putting away light blankets and adding richer colors and more blankets and throws, bringing in wool and cashmere alongside linen.

Autumn also means taking long, warm baths, one of the greatest ways to enjoy the cooler weather. I make the most of this ritual by drying aromatic herbs to scent the bath and soothe my skin.

In these pages, you'll find projects and ideas for getting ready for cooler weather and enjoying the change of seasons.

A Simple Patchwork

Using Fabric Remnants

At Fog Linen, we always have leftover fabric after we've cut what is needed for a pattern. At our factory in Lithuania, there are rooms filled with linen scraps of all colors and prints. It is my job (and one I wholeheartedly enjoy) to find ways to use them. Making use of these small pieces of fabric is both a way to be less wasteful and a chance to stretch myself creatively. I receive a few boxes at a time and start to plan. Often I use the remnants in one of my many patchwork projects, which I think of as part mental puzzle and part work of art.

Even if you don't have boxes of fabric scraps, there are almost always bits of material around the house that can be repurposed. Sometimes it's a favorite old shirt that is no longer being worn because of a stain. Or maybe it's from a linen sheet with a frayed or ripped edge. By cutting away the stained or ripped part and making small, uniformly shaped squares out of the rest, you will have the materials you need to create your own patchwork. Use the squares to make a cushion cover, a tote bag, a coverlet, or a curtain. I find that using fabric from old, well-loved items gives the patchwork more charm, but even if you use new fabric, your piece will still be artful and unique.

I typically select fabric scraps of the same color, but that is a personal preference. There are no rules for making patchwork. Your squares can be the same size, or you can make some larger and some smaller, which will create a more whimsical-looking patchwork.

above: A floor mat made from scraps of linen used in our products. I made this for my first book, *Linen Work*, almost twenty years ago. I've probably washed it one hundred times, and I still use it.

right: A curtain panel made by sewing together Fog Linen kitchen towels. I like to use towels from a single collection, in this case the 2019 Fall collection, so the colors and designs complement each other.

next page: A curtain for the kitchen pantry made with scraps of white linen of different thicknesses, some from sheets, others from kitchen towels, and still others from scarves.

A patchwork apron made
with recycled indigo-dyed
denim from Okayama Denim,
a store specializing in Japanese
selvedge denim.

Someya Suzuki, a Japanese textile company specializing in naturally dyed aprons and bags, makes beautiful patchwork products. They use a lot of recycled fabric scraps in their designs, like this *furoshiki* (wrapping cloth), which is made from Fog Linen fabric remnants and dyed by Someya Suzuki.

Patchwork Linen

This makes a 9 in [23 cm] square of patchwork. You can easily adapt this to fit the dimensions of your space by adding or subtracting rows of fabric pieces. You can use a single piece of linen or piece together smaller remnants of fabric in the same color palette. The suggested sizes of the scraps are just a guide. Feel free to cut them as you wish.

MATERIALS

One 15 in [38 cm] square of linen, or enough smaller pieces to add up to the same size

Rotary cutter or scissors

Sewing mat

Ruler

Straight pins

Sewing machine

Thread

Iron

1. Using the rotary cutter or scissors, along with the sewing mat and ruler, cut the fabric into twenty-two pieces: three 4 in [10 cm] squares, four 3½ in [9 cm] squares, four 3 in [7.5 cm] squares, five 2½ in [6 cm] squares, and six 2 in [5 cm] squares.

2. Arrange the pieces of fabric in a grid with five columns of squares. Pin two squares of the same size along one edge, then sew them together using a ¼ in [6 mm] seam allowance. Finish the seam with a zigzag stitch.

3. Working one column at a time, sew the pieces together into a strip. Finish each seam with a zigzag stitch. Repeat this process for all five columns of squares.

4. Use a hot iron to flatten the seam allowances to one side. Turn the piece right-side up and sew ⅛ in [4 mm] from the seam, so the seam allowance will lay flat.

5. Sew the five columns together, using a ¼ in [6 mm] seam allowance and finishing with a zigzag stitch. Use a hot iron to flatten the seam allowances to one side. Turn the fabric right-side up and sew ⅛ in [4 mm] from each seam, so the seam allowances will lay flat. Trim the fabric to make a 9 in [23 cm] square. You can repeat this process to make a patchwork of your desired size.

Creating a Small Oasis

Selecting Plants for the Garden

I grew up in Morioka, a city in the Tohoku region of northern Japan. It's a midsize city, surrounded by a river, forests, and mountains. I was not only close to nature but also lucky enough to have a large garden at home.

When my sister and I were little, our parents installed a large lawn in the middle of the garden. We played on the grass and napped on the hammock hung between the trees flanking the lawn. In the winter, my father piled the snow into a gentle slope for sledding. I have such fond memories of my childhood garden.

Once my sister and I left home, my parents replaced the lawn with dozens of varieties of roses and an herb garden. After I moved to Tokyo for college, my mom would visit, bringing me fragrant bouquets from the garden.

Living in the middle of Tokyo, it is hard to find a house with enough land for a garden like the one my parents had. For years, I made do

with potted plants, but when we moved into our new house, we finally had the space—about 160 sq ft [15 sq m]—for a little garden. We talked a lot about how to use this space, what kinds of plants would do well in our climate, and most importantly, what kind of garden we could realistically maintain, given our busy lives.

We ultimately decided that trees made the most sense, but even then, we had questions:

Are some trees "tidier," producing less leaf litter? Which ones are less prone to insect infestations and therefore require fewer pesticides? Which trees will look best in winter? Which trees produce fragrant flowers? How many trees can we plant in our small space and still leave room for a few raised beds for a kitchen herb garden?

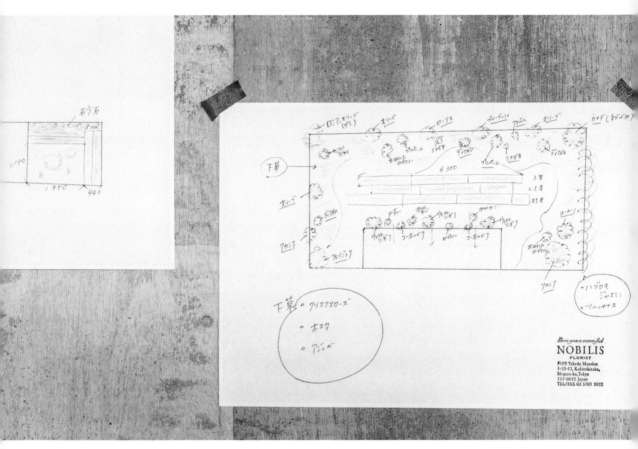

above: This garden sketch was done by Sachiko Shirakawa. She made sure there was a good balance of tall trees and shorter plants to make good use of the small space. The pink jasmine will soon grow to cover the fence.

above: We chose old railroad ties to delineate a path in the middle of the garden. They won't rot, even in the damp ground, and they haven't been treated with chemicals, which could leach into the soil.

We decided to enlist the help of a professional. Sachiko Shirakawa is a florist and the owner of Nobilis, a company that has delivered beautiful flowers to my store every week for the past few years. She's very knowledgeable about plants and offered to design our garden. Sachiko surprised me by recommending a list of plants native to, or common in, Australia. As Sachiko explained, climate change has increased the length and intensity of Tokyo summers. Many of the trees traditionally grown here respond to this extended period of heat by growing too tall and too fast; therefore they need a lot of maintenance and are more vulnerable to pests. Trees, both native and those introduced to Australia, are accustomed to longer periods of heat and strong sunlight and can handle this hotter climate in Tokyo.

Designing the garden didn't take much time for Sachiko. After listening to our requests, she presented us with sketches and plant lists. We decided on a mix of trees, shrubs, and perennial plants for our garden. For trees, we chose maple, acacia, olive, bay, and eucalyptus. For shrubs, we especially liked privet, mintbush, oakleaf hydrangea, ninebark, jasmine, and coastal rosemary bushes. And for perennials, we picked leopard plant, African lily, Christmas rose, ajuga, and plantain lily, a type of hosta.

After we decided on what we wanted, Sachiko traveled to find the best sources. And finally, on a nice fall day, we started our garden. The first step was to place, partly buried, old wooden railroad ties in the middle of the garden. These would serve as markers for a path. Around these, we planted the shrubs and smaller plants, and around those, the trees.

Now, every morning and evening, we spend time in the garden, watering and just enjoying the plants. It feels so nice to add more oxygen to the air and create a home for birds and insects, like the butterflies and dragonflies that flit around us on spring and summer mornings. And we are able to better observe the change in the seasons, which is reflected in the trees and plants. We greet them every morning and ask how they are; they feel like they are members of our family. The time we spend in the garden each morning, tending to our plants and watching them grow, brings me so much happiness and helps reduce my stress. Even if you don't have space for a garden, you can still find joy from plants and trees in pots. Check to see which plants thrive in your environment.

Air-Drying Vegetables

Getting the Most Flavor Out of Your Food

One beautiful and sunny morning I woke up early, the air was cool, and it felt like fall. The heat and humidity of the summer was gone and the sky was clear. I decided to go to my favorite vegetable market, a pleasant twenty-minute walk from my house. When I got there it was still quiet, with vendors setting up their stalls and making handmade signs with information about the fruits and vegetables for sale. The growers I talked with had so many great tips for preparing simple and delicious meals. I'm often surprised by how easy it is to cook with produce that is fresh and in season.

A visit to the vegetable market is now part of my weekend routine, which means I can incorporate the tastes of each season into my cooking. These weekly trips are made even sweeter by visiting Katane, the bakery next door, for a pastry and a cup of coffee after shopping.

One of the most exciting tips I've learned about cooking vegetables comes from Rika Maezawa, who owns a beautiful restaurant called Nanakusa and has a cookbook on the way. She suggests letting vegetables dry for a few hours and up to two days before cooking to intensify their flavors. As the vegetables lose some of their moisture, they become chewier and more easily take on any flavors added during cooking.

At first this sounded a bit odd to me, but as I thought about it, I realized how frequently I came across dried, or partially dried, vegetables in Japanese food. This is a fairly common practice for preserving foods, and has a long history in the cuisine.

Not only can you dry vegetables but also tofu and all kinds of fish and seafood, including bonito, shrimp, scallops, and squid. These dried foods show up everywhere in our day-to-day cooking. In addition to making them shelf-stable, drying foods can often intensify and concentrate their flavors, which makes them convenient and economical—only a little is needed, and they impart even more flavor than fresh versions.

VEGETABLES

This drying technique works with just about any vegetable, but here are a few good ones to experiment with:

Mushrooms

Onions, or any other root vegetable

Tomatoes

1. Tear the mushrooms into small pieces with your hands. Halve the onions (or other root vegetables) and tomatoes and cut into slices about ½ to 1 in [12 mm to 2.5 cm] thick. The idea is to create as much surface area as possible, so each piece dries evenly throughout.

2. Place the cut vegetables on a baking sheet or on large plates and set them in a sunny spot in your kitchen or, ideally, outside in a dry and warm area. Let the vegetables dry for a few hours or up to 2 days. Their texture will become chewy.

3. You can cook the vegetables as you normally would, though I particularly like to use them in miso soup, stir-fries, on pizza, or to make pickles.

above: One of the vendors makes these sweet bags from old newspapers.

above: Tear maitake mushrooms into small pieces by hand.

above: Thinly slice fibrous vegetables such as sweet potatoes, lotus roots, and pumpkin.

above: Just a few hours of drying will intensify the flavor of your vegetables.

New Harvest Rice

Appreciating Subtle Differences in Taste

There is a small rice shop in our neighborhood where they sell different varieties of rice from all over Japan. When I was child, there were only a couple of types of rice carried in stores: *Koshi hikari* and *Sasanishiki*, which are both short-grain varieties. These days, there are so many, some of them with cute names and packages showing cartoon character mascots. The descriptions almost make you forget they are all rice. This one is sweet and sticky; that one is shiny, with a robust flavor. It is like reading about coffee beans or wine.

I love having access to so much variety and go back each week to buy a new type of rice to experiment with—luckily the rice shop lets me buy small quantities. After I've selected my rice, the shop owner will ask how much of the bran I want left on when the rice is polished. The bran contains vitamins, but it makes the rice look brownish and taste chewier than white rice, which has no bran. Brown rice also takes longer to cook. Once I decide how much of the bran I would like, the owner puts the rice into a machine and polishes it to order.

Every October, the rice crop is harvested and shipped to stores. Even though rice is eaten throughout the year, the new harvest is special—lush, sweet, and plump. That is why we eat many more rice dishes in the fall. In the mornings, we get up a little bit earlier than usual to cook a pot of rice, which we eat with miso soup and homemade pickles. Depending on our mood, we might also add baked or grilled fish; *tamagoyaki*, Japanese egg omelets; *ohitashi*, vegetables cooked with dashi; or *natto*, fermented soybeans.

Fall is also a good time to change the vegetables and flavorings in miso soup. Sometimes it's seaweed; other times, it's clams, mushrooms, or tofu. There are so many possible variations. Together, rice and miso soup make a perfect breakfast.

After making breakfast, we'll use the leftover rice to make rice balls for lunch. Fillings might include *umeboshi*, or pickled plum; *okaka*, or bonito flakes; *mentaiko*, or pollack roe; and *sake*, or salmon.

above: This may look like a lot of food, but it's a fairly typical breakfast spread, which gives us energy and a good start to the day. It will include a bowl of rice, miso soup, pickles, folded egg omelet, boiled spinach, little fishes, and grated daikon radish.

above: I have an electric rice cooker, but I recently bought a Kinto brand ceramic cooker for gas stoves. It cooks rice perfectly, and in a short time. I also like its simple shape.

Hand-Carved Wooden Spoon

Rediscovering Traditional Handicrafts

My mother used to do wood carving at home, sometimes adding decorative details to furniture that my father made, sometimes making small pieces of her own design, like coasters, little dishes, and trays. I love the things she made—and the fact that she made them. Many of these pieces are in my home today. As a kid, though, I never had much interest in doing any woodworking. My school offered lots of classes, including one on wood block printing, but none of these held any appeal for me. My attitude changed a few years ago when I had the opportunity to participate in an all-day workshop with a very well-respected artist, Ryuji Mitani. It was focused on making wooden spoons, and it turned out to be an incredible and fully immersive experience.

One Saturday, very early in the morning, I drove to the city of Matsumoto, which is about four hours west of Tokyo. I arrived in Mr. Mitani's workshop around nine. There were ten other people taking the workshop, and we all boarded a small bus and rode to a tiny mountain town. Once there, we walked for another half an hour, until we reached a small clearing. We sat under the trees alongside a river while Mr. Mitani explained how to carve a spoon.

First we sketched the outline of a spoon on a rectangular piece of wood. Then, with a chisel, we began cutting away the wood around the outline.

We worked happily with the sounds of the river in the background. After about two hours, our blocks of wood began to resemble actual spoons—with a little help along the way from Mr. Mitani. When we were done, we went back to Mr. Mitani's workshop, where he served us warm soup, bread, salad, and wine. We all used our newly carved spoons to eat. As I discovered, wood carving is both meditative and creatively fulfilling. I've since made several other hand-carved utensils, including a mate for that first spoon.

right: A few of the many wooden items in my collection—some old, some made by me, and some made by craftspeople whose work I love.

You can use any hardwood to make the spoon. Just make sure it is dry, seasoned wood, rather than freshly cut.

MATERIALS

**Rectangular piece of hardwood
approximately 2 by 7½ by 1 in [5 by 19 by 2.5 cm]**

Pencil

Small saw, around 10 in [25 cm]

Wood-carving knife

Chisel

Spoon gouge

320-grit sandpaper

180-grit sandpaper

120-grit sandpaper

Wood rasp (optional)

Small rag

**Food-safe oil, such as sesame, walnut, or tung
(but not olive oil, which becomes rancid)**

1. Place the piece of wood on a flat surface and, using a pencil, draw the outline of the spoon you'd like to carve directly onto your piece of wood.

2. Cut around this shape using a small saw, carving knife, or chisel. You may need to alternate between the tools.

3. Hold the spoon in your lap, or clamp it down on a worktable. With the gouge, carve out the bowl of the spoon. Start with small cuts. If you're making a cooking spoon, the bowl does not need to be very deep. If you'd like to make a spoon to eat with, it should be a bit deeper. Either way, work incrementally so you don't inadvertently carve too deeply.

4. Once the inside of the bowl is roughly carved out, shape the edge and back of the bowl with the wood-carving knife. Then refine the back.

5. The handle is the last part of the spoon to be carved. With the bowl side facing up, begin shaving strips of wood all the way down the spoon to the end of the handle. Work incrementally again to avoid taking off too much wood. If you have a rasp, it can help to get a rounded edge, but you can just use your carving knife.

6. Returning to the bowl of the spoon, continue to carve out small bits at a time to get a smooth surface with as few ridges as possible.

7. Once you're happy with the shape of your spoon, it's time to sand. Start with the roughest grade sandpaper and move to smoother grits to give the spoon a final sanding.

8. Finally, dampen the end of a small rag with food-safe oil and oil your spoon. Let your spoon cure for 1 to 2 hours before using.

Japanese Bath

Relaxing at the End of the Day

Japan has a very rich bathing culture with roots in sixth-century Buddhism. Taking a bath and ritualistically cleaning the body was one of the most important parts of life for Buddhist monks. They believed that bathing would fight seven diseases and in turn, give the bather seven blessings, so many temples offered worshippers a place to bathe.

Neighborhood public baths in Japan, called *sento*, date back to a time when most people lacked a place to bathe at home. However, the tradition has endured, even though most Japanese homes now have bathtubs. There are still traditional sento in residential areas, and larger and more deluxe ones, known as "supersento," have sprung up through-out Japan. *Onsen*, natural hot springs with adjoining bathhouses, are also very popular throughout the country. These are usually in mountain towns, but not always. Often, these onsen are near traditional inns, called *ryokan*, where the cost of the room includes all meals. Visiting a ryoken feels like the ultimate luxury, and I try to go at least a few times a year.

At home, I take a bath every morning and every night. Bathing at night is a common practice in Japan, a way to remove the grime of the city and relax our bodies and minds before bed. I believe bathing has real physical benefits, including improved circulation and a more settled nervous system. A bath acts as a mini-massage for our internal organs, and relaxes muscles and joints, relieving stiffness.

Now that I have an herb garden at home, I'm able to use both fresh and dried herbs in the bath. I make bath salts with a blend of dried herbs, flowers, and aromatics, such as mint, rosemary, rose geranium, and lemongrass. I use fruits and vegetables as well, including my favorite, yuzu, a type of citrus with a heady scent. Yuzu has a warming quality—perfect for when you feel a cold coming on. I also slice ginger and add that to the bath, sometimes with a splash of wine or sake. This may sound strange, but I find it very warming for cold nights or mornings.

Here are a few easy recipes for making bath salts at home. Epsom salt is a soothing condi-tioner for the skin, but it's optional. Feel free to experiment with whatever you have at home: Dried rose petals, rosemary, mint, and thyme would all make pleasant-smelling bath salts.

left: Mint and rose geranium collected from the rooftop garden.

above: Herbal bouquet picked in the garden and added to the bath.

next page: Freshly picked herbs and fruit for the bath. There are no rules; you can pick as much or as little you like, in any combination that suits you.

Lavender Bath Salts

MAKES 1 TO 2 CUPS [250 TO 450 G]

1 cup [250 g] sea salt or Himalayan pink salt
1 cup [200 g] Epsom salt (optional)
1 Tbsp dried lavender
3 or 4 drops lavender essential oil (optional)

Combine the sea salt, Epsom salt, if using, and dried lavender in a medium bowl and mix well. Add the lavender oil, if using, one drop at a time, and stir to combine. Transfer to a small glass jar with a lid. To use, add 3 to 4 spoonfuls of the salts to your bath. The salts should last, tightly sealed, for 3 to 4 months.

Yuzu Bath Salts

MAKES 1 TO 2 CUPS [250 TO 450 G]

Peel of 1 medium yuzu or other citrus, like Meyer lemon
1 cup [250 g] sea salt or Himalayan pink salt
1 cup [200 g] Epsom salt (optional)

Chop the peel into a fine dice. Transfer to a medium bowl and add the sea salt and Epsom salt, if using. Mix well.

Transfer the bath salts to a small glass jar with a lid. To use, add 3 to 4 spoonfuls of the salts to your bath. The salts should last, tightly sealed, for 3 to 4 months.

Handmade Soap

Making your own soap is economical and satisfying. And since you are choosing your own aromatics, you can consider which properties are most important to you. I use dried marigold because of its beautiful color and anti-inflammatory effects (it's great if you have sunburned skin), and lavender essential oil for its calming and pain-reducing properties. You can add whichever dried flowers, herbs, and scents most appeal to you.

MAKES 1 BAR OF SOAP

One 1¾ oz [50 g] chunk unscented glycerin soap

Pinch of dried marigold, other herbs or flowers of your choice (preferably organic), or herbal tea

3 or 4 drops essential oil of your choice, or a blend of your favorites

Coat a mold or a short glass, 3 to 4 in [7.5 to 10 cm] in diameter, with vegetable oil. Place a heat-resistant glass bowl or beaker in a pot of simmering water. Cut the glycerin soap into small chunks and transfer to the bowl. Stir, allowing the soap to melt completely.

Add the dried herbs or flowers and essential oil and stir to combine. Remove from the heat and pour the mixture into the prepared mold. Allow to cool completely, 1 to 2 hours.

Remove the soap from the mold and use immediately or store in a cool place for up to 5 months.

 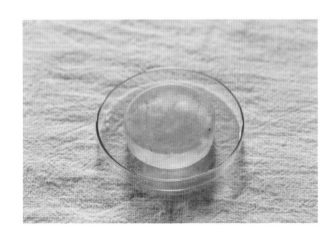

WINTER

Growing up in snow country in far northern Japan has left me with many good memories of winter. We filled the long, cold winters with skiing, ice skating, and playing in the snow. We would return from the outdoors to a toasty warm and cozy house. My grandmother had a *kotatsu*, a low table with an electric heater underneath, usually covered with a heavy quilted blanket. We would spend hours sitting on the tatami mat with our legs tucked underneath the table, playing card games and eating mikan oranges, the satsuma mandarins (similar to tangerines) that grow abundantly in Japan in the cold winter months.

Winter meals brought even more warmth to the table. We often cooked *sukiyaki*, shabu-shabu, and many different kinds of nabe right in the dining room on a portable stove placed on the table. These foods always feel cozy to me, with their steam and good smells filling the room and warming us from the inside out.

December is the busiest month in Japan. In fact, it's often called *Shiwasu*, which roughly translates as "master" and "to run." In other words, it's so busy that a priest has to pray on the run. Much of the busyness comes from shopping for *Oseibo*, the year-end gifts we give to family, friends, and, most important, the people we do business with. End-of-year parties, called *bounenkai*, are also traditional for Japanese companies.

December is also the time to prepare for the New Year. We put up decorations at gates and entryways, and prepare foods for the New Year's Day celebrations, sometimes weeks in advance. An important part of the end-of-year preparations is a deep and ritualistic cleaning of the house and office. The purpose is to clear the space not just of dirt and clutter but also of bad spirits and emotional heaviness.

In this section, I share some of my own winter traditions: How I bring more warmth to my house, the New Year's foods I love to make, and my own version of cleaning for the New Year.

Preparing the House for Winter

Layering Textiles for Warmth and Comfort

Winter in Tokyo comes suddenly; the mild, sweater-weather days of November end abruptly around the start of December. The temperature drops, and I can feel a cold wind when I step out into my little garden. The first one to get ready for the colder weather is our cat, whose normally short hair transforms into a long, thick coat.

This was our first winter in our new house, and I began preparing for the change in seasons by taking winter clothes out of boxes and packing away T-shirts and light dresses. I then moved on to the dining room, where I hung curtains over the windows, and on to the bedrooms, where I replaced the light comforters with heavier ones and added more blankets.

What I don't change, however, are the linen sheets and blankets. While people often think of linen as a warm-weather fabric, it's just as appropriate for the colder months. The natural fibers of linen, specifically the spaces in the fibers, hold body heat extremely well—much better than many synthetics. And linen comes in many different weaves and treatments; some are heavier, and some have a brushed surface, which gives them an even softer feel.

One of the ways I make the house feel warmer is by covering the floor with various textiles, including kantha quilts, which I recently started importing from India to sell in my stores. These are made from scraps of recycled saris and dhotis, which are stitched together to make a patchwork. The top and bottom are different colors, and I can change which side faces up depending on my mood or to match the color of the tablecloth. It feels cozy to sit on the floor with blankets and cushions, which reminds me of sitting around the kotatsu heater at my grandparents' house.

left: A kantha quilt in warm tones placed underneath the dining table. In the winter, I often get bunches of these red flowers, called *Mayumi*, for the table because they make the room feel warm and cozy.

above: Since we don't have kids at home, Christmas decorations at our house are very simple. I group arrangements of wood and metal ornaments on the shelf. Some of them were given to us by friends; others I've collected myself.

Organizing the Closet
Folding Techniques and Getting Rid of Unused Items

When I was in college, I had summer jobs at a few different clothing stores. Each store had its own way of folding clothes. Since it was my responsibility to keep the shelves looking neat and tidy, I learned the best way to fold shirts, pants, and scarves. After customers tried on clothes, I would refold and reshelve them. By the time I graduated, I was an expert folder.

I still get a lot of satisfaction out of folding clothes, especially finding the perfect shape for each item. In my stores, I start each morning by checking the shelves and refolding clothes and scarves. This not only makes the products look good but also uses the shelf space in the most efficient way. I do this at home too, sometimes to the bewilderment of my boyfriend, who cares a bit less about drawer and shelf organization!

I believe there is something intrinsic to Japanese culture about folding. We learn origami at a very young age. And then there's furoshiki, the cloth that's folded around gifts, especially for formal occasions. A kimono, the most traditional clothing item in Japan, requires a very precise method of folding.

Folding clothes carefully also helps keep them in their best condition, prolonging their life.

Here are examples of how I've tackled clothes storage in my house.

Of course, when you go through your closets and drawers to refold items, you can also decide whether you're holding on to clothes you no longer wear. I like doing this in December as part of my annual house cleaning because I'm in the right frame of mind to evaluate what I want to keep in my life and what I'm ready to get rid of. If I haven't worn something for at least year, I usually let it go. And there are some things that just never get worn; even if I liked the color or cut, for some reason they just didn't work on my body, or I didn't like the feel of the fabric. I often hold on to these items, expecting to use them, and the end of the year is a good time to reevaluate. Once I've pulled out all the clothes, bags, and shoes I don't use, I take them to the flea market to sell or donate them to a used clothing store.

I find it so much easier to get dressed once I've pared down my closet. With a more limited wardrobe, I can see what I have and coordinate my clothing with belts, scarves, tights, and shoes. And when there is less, I appreciate so much more the things that I do have.

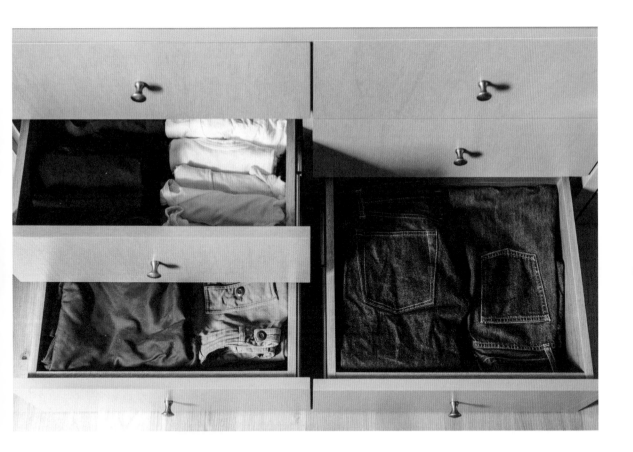

left: I added these wooden dividers to the dresser drawers so small things like handkerchiefs, belts, and socks each have their own dedicated space and don't get jumbled together.

above: When folding larger objects like pants and jeans, I try to use the full length of the drawer. I fold T-shirts so they use the full height of the drawer, and stack them in several rows from front to back to prevent the drawers from getting messy.

next spread: We use an old writing bureau as a dresser in the guest room. The drawers are stocked with things overnight visitors might need: towels, extra blankets and sheets, even a spare set of pajamas.

Decorating for Christmas

Making a Simple Wreath with a Hanger and Brass Ring

Even though Japan doesn't have a Christian tradition, Christmas has become a very popular holiday. I've loved celebrating Christmas ever since I was a child—I even believed in Santa Claus until I was ten. Luckily, our house had a chimney, which helped keep the Santa myth alive. Beyond my excitement at waking up and finding the presents I had asked for on Christmas morning, I loved decorating the house for the season. I still love making decorations to display around the house.

In addition to homemade ornaments, I always hang wreaths with fresh greenery. This year, I wanted to try making my own with plants from the garden. I came up with a few simple ideas using brass rings, scarf hangers, and a star ornament. You can adapt the instructions below according to what you have around your house, or what you can find easily at the local craft shop or florist.

A wreath makes a very nice gift. A friend sent us one made from greenery picked from her garden, and we were delighted with it.

MATERIALS
2 to 3 evergreen branches, about 2 ft [60 cm] each
Brass ring about 8½ in [21.5 cm] in diameter
Scarf hanger
Thin twine or strong thread
Scissors
Star-shaped ornament

1. Arrange the greens around the brass ring until you're happy with the shape.

2. Using the twine or thread, tie the greens around the ring at 3 in [7.5 cm] intervals so they are securely attached.

3. Attach the hanger to the top of the ring, and hang the ornament from the top of the wreath so it dangles down in the center.

Growing Plants
from Seeds and Scraps

An Experiment with Indoor Gardening

A few years ago, I left an avocado pit on the counter, partly out of neglect and partly because I liked its perfect round shape. After a week or two, I noticed a few small shoots coming from the pit and decided to give it a bit of water. A few days later, I placed it in a shallow bowl filled with water and watched the roots continue to grow. Another few weeks, and I was curious to see how far I could take this experiment. I planted the gangly pit in the tiny garden space behind my old house in Tokyo, and to my absolute surprise, it grew and grew, eventually reaching nearly 9 ft [3 m]!

This experience sparked a kind of fascination with how much energy is contained in plants—even the discarded scraps. Watching potatoes sprout in the vegetable drawer of my refrigerator, or even the decorative leaves from the florist sending roots into a vase of water—there's so much life left in these plants, it seems a shame to discard them prematurely. Now I plant leftover seeds from the fruit we eat in our rooftop garden. And I regrow carrots from their tops. I just place the tops in water and in about a week they sprout new leaves. Then I plant them in soil for the next harvest.

Growing vegetables from scraps isn't foolproof. Sometimes the shoots take off, and sometimes they don't. But I love watching the growing process, especially in the winter, when it's nice to bring more life indoors.

Left to right, top to bottom: Pineapple, limes, pears, kabocha squash, avocado, persimmons, and carrots—a few of the fruits and vegetables from my table, which I've propagated indoors. Even if I'm not successful in regrowing them, I appreciate the inherent beauty of the seeds.

above: The branches we cut from the dracaena
growing at our house are now sending out roots.

above: A few burgeoning plants grown from seed:
a persimmon, a lemon, and an avocado.

New Year's Party Foods

Making Vegetable Sushi

There are so many parties and gatherings during the weeks leading up to Christmas, and then between Christmas and New Year's—sometimes several per week. As fun as these get-togethers are, I often feel run down and a bit heavy after eating rich, meaty, and fried party foods for several weeks in a row. Thinking ahead to my own end-of-year party for Fog Linen, I wanted to put together a lighter menu that would still feel festive and fun.

There's a little sushi restaurant in my neighborhood with beautiful displays of fresh vegetables in the glass case instead of the more standard fish. The chef, Mr. Horikawa, uses the same precise and exacting techniques typically applied to conventional sushi to create delicious rolls and nigiri made almost exclusively from seasonal vegetables

and fruit. I love this approach and often stop by for a few bites of sushi and a glass of sake for dinner. It occurred to me that vegetable sushi is a perfect thing to make at home, since finding and storing sushi-grade fish can be difficult for the home cook. Shopping for seasonal vegetables is much more manageable.

I liked the idea of making our company party interactive, so I decided to ask Mr. Horikawa if he would be willing to come and teach us how to make a few of his favorite kinds of vegetable sushi. Happily, he agreed. We cooked the sushi rice and prepped the vegetables so guests would have everything they needed to assemble their sushi. Mr. Horikawa showed us a few simple techniques, and then everybody was free to experiment with putting together their own combinations. It was perfect—a simple, beautiful, and healthful party spread.

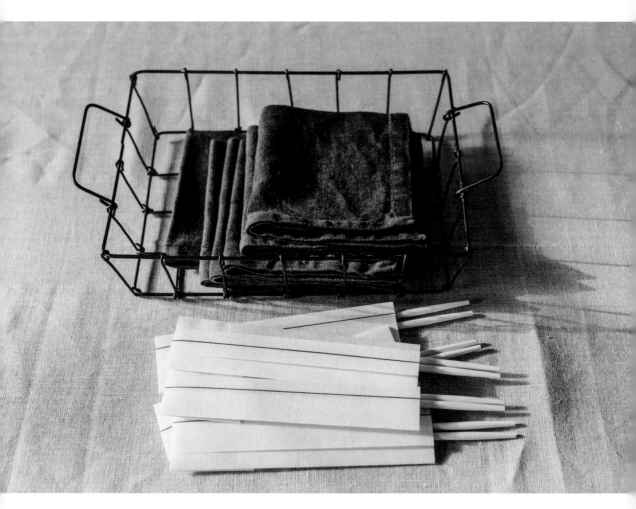

above: Linen napkins and disposable wooden chopsticks wrapped in hand-made washi paper wrappers.

above: Guests pick their own sake cups
from the bamboo basket. Sake is served
from shallow porcelain pourers.

above: A platter of finished sushi, including, clockwise from left: daikon radish shoots with natto; *menegi*, or bunching onion; boiled *mizuna*; roasted eggplant; lightly charred green pepper; steamed *nanohana* (similar to broccolini); cooked red pepper; roasted shiitake mushroom; myoga and quail egg; shallot and quail egg.

right: Mr. Horikawa demonstrates the best way to form sushi. He starts with cooked rice seasoned with red rice vinegar and a little sugar, forms it gently in his hand, and tops it with a variety of cooked and seasoned vegetables.

next spread (left): Shiitake mushroom; green pepper; red pepper; nanohana (similar to broccolini); myoga and quail egg; shallot and quail egg; menegi, or bunching onion; daikon radish shoots with natto.

next spread (right): Wasabi root roll; diced aonori seaweed and wasabi roll; mountain yam and pickled plum roll; pickled daikon; mountain yam, ginger, and turnip, all pickled and thinly sliced; sliced Le Lectier pear topped with wasabi; muscat grapes with wasabi; kiwi with wasabi.

Cleaning the House for the New Year

The Japanese Custom of Oosouji

Just before the very end of the year, many Japanese people do a deep cleaning of their houses to welcome the New Year. This ritual, called *oosouji*, dates back to the eighth-century Heian period, when it was known as *susu harai*. The deep cleaning was accompanied by placing pairs of pine branches, or *kadomatsu*, at the front gate. All of this was done in anticipation of a visit from Toshigami-sama, the god of the new year, who, according to legend, would go from house to house on December 31 bestowing good fortune and giving everyone the gift of another year of life. When the house is clean and ready for the new year, a braided straw rope called a *shimekazari* is placed across the top of the entrance.

Oosouji is more than just cleaning and decluttering; it's about letting go of unwanted things, bringing order to chaos, and welcoming the new year with a clean slate. Businesses practice oosouji too. It's a chance to close up accounts, archive old files, and even resolve outstanding conflicts. Even schoolchildren perform oosouji by cleaning out their desks and backpacks.

In oosouji, there is a focus on minimalism, on cultivating a more pleasing environment with fewer things, but ones that have more meaning and significance. At our office, when we start making plans for December, the first thing we mark on the calendar is our cleaning day. On the last workday in December, everyone arrives in jeans and T-shirts, and we clean the office from top to bottom. It feels so good to clean with everyone working together, knowing that once we've finished , we've also finished our work for the year.

At home, I usually try to do my end-of-year cleaning little by little every weekend during the month of December. Recently, I've decided that I want to make my cleaning more environmentally friendly by using natural cleansers, like the peels of mikan oranges, apples, and other fruit, instead of synthetic detergents. Orange peels have an oil call limonene and apple peels have malic acid, both of which cut through grease and condition wood surfaces. These natural cleansers smell fresh and are safe for kids and pets.

You can easily make your own fruit-peel cleaners. For a homemade orange cleaner, in a small saucepan, combine the peel of 1 orange for every ½ cup [120 ml] of water. Bring this to a boil and then simmer for 15 minutes. Once it cools, transfer to a clean spray bottle. It will keep for up to 1 month. Use throughout the kitchen and on wood.

For apple peels, the process is even easier. Using a large piece of fresh apple peel, wipe down the inside of your sink or countertops. You can also add apple peels, along with a bit of water, to dirty or stained aluminum pots. Just boil this mixture for 15 minutes or so. It will cut through even baked-on grease.

Making Miso

A Staple in Japanese Cooking

Fermented foods feature prominently in Japanese cuisine, both in popularity and variety, but the one that is used most often is miso. Miso is made with rice that has been inoculated with a type of mold, called koji. When combined with cooked soybeans, the rice koji helps facilitate a second fermentation. The resulting beneficial bacteria are good for the gut and, I believe, for one's general health and longevity. Rice koji is available from a number of online sources.

Traditionally, families make miso using a starter from the previous year's batch. This creates a kind of resident bacteria specific to each home. Miso is usually made in January, the coldest time of the year. There is an old saying that water in the cold months is good medicine, good for body and mind. So making miso with the coldest water makes it doubly healthy. The cold weather also helps slow fermentation and allows for more of the soybean flavor to be extracted, resulting in a richer-tasting miso.

Miso is the basis for miso soup, can be used as a dip for vegetables, and makes a great marinade, which I like to use on cheese. I cut cream cheese into small cubes, cover them well with a mixture of 1½ Tbsp of miso and 1 Tbsp of mirin, and let sit for 12 to 24 hours. The cheese is delicious spread on toast or crackers, accompanied by wine or sake.

You'll need a large enamel pot or a glass jar with a wide mouth for storing the miso. Keep in mind that it takes about 1 year for the miso to ferment.

MAKES ABOUT 6 LB [2.7 KG]

1¼ cups [250 g] dried soybeans
1¼ cups [250 g] rice koji
½ cup [120 g] kosher salt, plus more for storing
Vodka or shochu, for wiping the pot

Rinse the soybeans thoroughly and transfer to a large pot. Add enough cold water to cover the beans by 2 to 3 in [5 to 7.5 cm], at least 4 cups [960 ml]. Soak for at least 18 hours. When ready to use, the soybeans will have doubled in size.

Drain the beans, return them to the pot, and add fresh water, covering them again by 2 to 3 in [5 to 7.5 cm]. Bring the beans to a boil, lower the heat, and simmer gently for 3 to 4 hours. The soybeans are ready when you can easily mash them between your thumb and index finger. Drain the beans and set aside just briefly.

While the beans are still hot, crush them with a mortar and pestle until only a few chunks remain. Alternatively, pulse them in a food processor, which will speed up the process. Transfer them to a large shallow bowl and let cool to room temperature.

In a medium bowl, mix together the rice koji and salt. Using your hands, mix until you feel a bit of moisture being released. Transfer the mixture to the bowl with the cooled soybeans and knead until well combined and uniform in consistency. This process will facilitate good fermentation.

Soak a few paper towels in vodka or shochu and wipe down the inside of the enamel pot or glass jar in which you'll store the miso in order to kill any unwanted bacteria. Using your hands, form tennis ball–size rounds of bean mash. One by one, throw the rounds firmly into the pot or jar. Press down on each ball as firmly as possible to remove any air pockets. This will prevent unwanted mold growth. Pat down the surface of the mash with the flat of your palm to make one unified mass.

Cover the miso mash with plastic wrap, making sure it lays directly on the surface of the mash all the way to the edge. Place about 2 cups [500 g] of salt in an even layer directly on top of the mash. Cover the pot with more plastic wrap or secure the jar with a tight-fitting lid.

Set the bean paste aside in a cool area, away from direct sunlight, without too much fluctuation in temperature. Fermentation is complete in 10 to 12 months. When ready, the miso will have turned a darker brown. If you find the surface is covered with mold, don't worry; just scrape it off.

Uncover the miso, discard the salt layer and plastic wrap, mix well, and enjoy! The miso will keep, covered, in the refrigerator for about 1 year.

SPRING

At the beginning of March, newspapers start issuing the cherry blossom forecast for the season: when we should expect to see the beautiful pink buds emerge and how numerous the blossoms might be. This always makes me feel antsy for spring, and even if there is a still a cold wind blowing, cherry blossoms signal that spring is close by.

In my neighborhood, there is a little path by a river surrounded by cherry trees. I walk this path every day to and from the office. Once the cherry blossom forecast is out, I begin checking these trees each morning. I watch as the buds begin forming, then grow, and finally burst into bloom.

The city, gray and flat at the tail end of winter, comes to life with the arrival of the blossoms, imbued with a pink light. It's easy to miss the cherry trees when they're not in bloom, but for those first weeks at the start of spring, the whole city is covered by their canopy. It's a magical time to visit Japan. And, if you happen to be flying to Japan during the cherry blossom season, be sure to sit by the window, where you will have a spectacular view.

Spring is also a time for renewed business activity. Both private companies and government agencies treat spring as the start of the fiscal year and hire new employees, whom they call freshman. And spring is the start of the new school year, bringing many new students into towns and cities. All of this makes for more bustle and activity as public spaces reawaken with the influx of people and the good energy they bring.

As for my own business, there is a noticeable increase in activity as people rediscover their love of linen with the approach of warmer weather. I can't blame them; I start wearing more linen in the spring too. We bring out a new line of clothes for spring, when our customers are eager for the chance to cast off heavy coats in favor of light and breathable fabrics.

This is also a time when I think about revamping my own wardrobe, dyeing old clothes and making something new, like a scarf.

A Capsule Wardrobe

Paring Down a Closet to Reveal More Possibilities

I have a very pared down closet. For spring, a linen coat, a few shirts, and a couple pairs of pants, all in just a few colors. During colder months, a few sweaters and warmer layers. On weekdays, these create the basis for my uniform, and I relish its simplicity. I used to approach dressing very differently. I was always collecting clothes—sometimes brand new, sometimes from secondhand shops—and packing them into an already overstuffed closet. I would often rediscover a long-buried article of clothing, as if excavated from a tomb. Clothing for all seasons was jumbled together, yet I never seemed to have anything to wear.

Now, rather than keeping the same assortment of clothes year-round, adding in some warmer pieces in the colder months and lighter ones for warmer weather, I start fresh each season. I assemble a small collection of items and purchase a few new things to augment what I have. When I start noticing a real change in weather—or I feel the urge to usher one in—I box up my closet and assemble the new season's collection.

I wash my clothes after each use. Sometimes I wear the same things a few times a week, though I try to style them differently to keep my outfits interesting. Part of what makes this approach work is retraining myself to buy fewer things. But there is also a kind of formula I apply to my seasonal capsule wardrobe.

1. Limit the color palette: If I frequently wear blue jeans, I try to pair these with shirts and tops in various shades of blue.

2. Buy clothes made from natural materials like linen, cotton, and wool. These breathable fabrics are not only more comfortable to wear but also hold up better year after year.

3. Invest in a long linen coat: A mid-thigh linen duster pulls just about any outfit together and can even double as a dress. Whenever I'm in a clothing rut and can't think of what to wear, a long linen coat always seems to be the answer.

4. Embrace a more lived-in look: For me, the beauty of linen is that it looks good even when it's not perfectly pressed. I let my linen clothes air dry after washing, which only enhances the natural drape of the fabric.

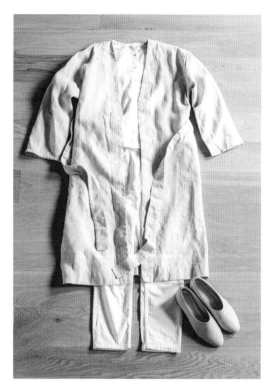

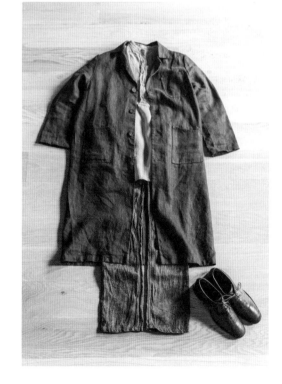

above: Fog Linen coats in four colors. These are my
uniform during the work week—I wear them all the time!

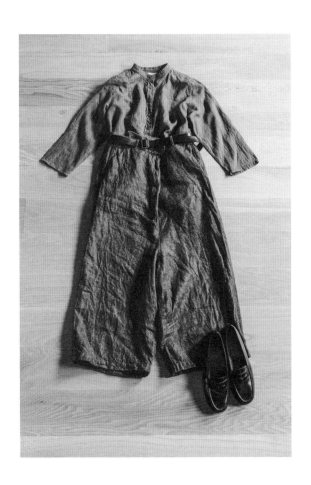

above: My solution to styling is staying within a single tone. Choose similar colors for tops and bottoms to make your outfits stylish and easy to mix and match.

Making a Scarf

An Easy Project to Brighten Your Wardrobe

I love scarves, and it will probably come as no surprise that most of the ones in my collection are linen. Frequently, when I have leftover linen, I'll use it to make a scarf. I love the drape of a linen scarf and the fact that it gets softer with each wash.

Recently, I've begun importing an array of cotton fabrics, including a thin cotton from India, and using these to make scarves and other items. The cotton used to make *lungi*, the sarong-like garment worn in India and elsewhere in Asia, traditionally comes in a blue checked pattern. As I've traveled in southern India visiting the factories where lungi are made, I've discovered hundreds of variations in the color palette and pattern. I now sell many products made from this and other high-quality cottons from India under my "miiThaii" label.

These thin cottons look beautiful layered against linen tops and dresses. And, like linen, they hold up well to washing and repeated wear, and look good even when they're wrinkled. A scarf is one of the easiest and most satisfying projects to make if you're new to sewing. It's a great feeling to be able to wear something you've made yourself.

This is a simple scarf with a fringed edge. Feel free to use any fabric you have, but loosely woven, thinner cloth will be a bit easier to work with. For printed fabrics, make sure the pattern is the same on both sides.

Cut the fabric to your desired length and width. One way to determine the right amount of fabric is to wrap it around your neck as you'd like to wear it. The width of the fabric will determine how full the scarf will look.

MATERIALS

One 1½ to 2 yd [1.4 to 1.8 m] piece of fabric

Sewing shears or fabric cutter

Ruler

Chalk pencil

Straight pins

Sewing machine or needle

Thread

1. Begin by cutting clean, straight edges on the long and short sides of your fabric using the ruler and the shears or fabric cutter.

2. Make the fringes: With the ruler and chalk pencil, draw a line about 2 in [5 cm] from the edge of each short end of the fabric.

3. Using the shears or a fabric cutter, pull away at the loose horizontal threads until you reach the marked line, creating a frayed edge.

4. Pull together a clump of the loosened threads. Dip your fingers in water and twist the threads until they form a tassel. Repeat this every ½ in [12 mm] along the two frayed edges.

5. Finally, hem the long edges of the scarf. To do this with a sewing machine, fold over each edge about ½ in [12 mm], pin in place, and sew a line of zigzag stitches along the edge to secure it. Or hem it by hand.

above: A few examples for how scarves, in different colors and tied in different styles, can dress up a simple shirt.

Dyeing Old Clothes

A Quick Fix for Worn-Out Garments

Recently, when I took some of my favorite spring clothes out of winter storage , I discovered they were covered with stains and yellowish discolorations. Since they had been sitting for many months, it was impossible to remove the stains, so I did what I had often seen my mother do in the same situation: I dyed them. It turned out to a very simple project, and the clothes, which otherwise would have been ruined, looked transformed and nearly new.

The process for dyeing is incredibly easy. I just mix a spoonful of salt with a packet of Dylon permanent dye and add it to a sink filled with hot water. I add the clothes and leave to soak for about 40 minutes. Then I rinse with water and let them air dry. You'll have the best results if you use a color a few shades darker than the original. I've found dyeing works as well on patterned clothes as it does on solids. Once you gain confidence, you can even try more playful techniques like tie-dyeing.

If your article of clothing has white or light-colored polyester thread, be aware that it might not hold the color of the dye. This can create an interesting and appealing look, as long as it doesn't come as a surprise.

Spring Arrangements

Filling Your Space with Flowers

I love having fresh flowers around. I get a weekly delivery of flowers for my Tokyo store from florist Sachiko Shirakawa. She has a great eye for beautiful and unusual arrangements. I always learn so much from her about different varieties and unique and interesting pairings.

Sachiko's flowers inspire me to create my own arrangements at home. I'll go into the garden and cut a few branches, especially in the spring, when there are new buds and flowers. But even a delicately shaped broad leaf or two can make a dramatic arrangement. To complement such pared-down arrangements, I find that unusual vessels work well. I'll repurpose objects from around the house and garden like cans, baskets, bottles, or even shallow bowls that might make an interesting vase. I can't take credit for this idea. It was the sixteenth-century tea master Sen no Rikyū who popularized the use of unexpected objects in flower arranging. He used fishermen's baskets as flower vases, something that has now become iconic in ikebana, the Japanese style of flower arranging. I channel his spirit as I dig up watering cans, pots, and old glasses to use as vessels.

The tradition of ikebana goes back to the seventh century. You're probably most familiar with one style of ikebana: spare arrangements with just one flower or a few types and a very structured, almost sculptural look. But there are many styles of ikebana, some with fuller and more loosely styled arrangements. Practitioners explain ikebana as the art of subtraction; it's not just the flowers that are appreciated, but also the empty spaces around and between them. There is an emphasis placed on restraint and the overall form of the arrangement. Without any cultural context, ikebana can seem excessively minimalist, but it makes more sense when you consider where these arrangements were traditionally placed—in the *tokonoma*, or alcoves in houses. They were considered to be two-dimensional, rather than three. This is quite different than a vase of flowers placed in the center of a table, where it is appreciated from many different angles.

I find beauty in just about every arrangement, whether it's a single bud in a small glass, a vase of abundant and wild flowers, or just some branches and leaves from the garden.

right: A traditional ikebana arrangement with daffodils, Japanese rose, *Leucocoryne*, and Japanese silverleaf placed in a tofu basket.

above: Branches with white and pink magnolia flowers just beginning to bud make a dramatic arrangement in a sturdy laboratory beaker.

above: A bunch of tulips allowed to follow their natural form.

above: A collection of small spring flowers,
including Persian buttercup, lachenalia, *Cerinthe*,
and fritillaria, arranged in various little jars.

above: A repurposed teapot holds a sweet arrangement
of violets and rosemary.

above: A wild and unruly arrangement made from branches and flowers from my garden. This one includes eucalyptus, mimosa, Russian olive, Christmas rose, euphorbia, and potato vine. I look for subtle pops of color to stand out against the shades of green.

Teatime

Japanese Tea and Seasonal Sweets

I've always embraced the practice of the coffee break. When I've finished a project, or just need to step away from my work, I'll get up and brew a pot of coffee. It's a good chance to stretch my legs and reset my brain, and I can usually eke out another few hours of work afterward. Increasingly though, I've replaced the coffee with green tea—either matcha, hojicha, or sencha, and serve that along with some sweets or little snacks. It's become one of my favorite rituals.

Tea ceremony is a beautiful tradition with a long history in Japan, but it's quite formal and has many rules. The tea used in formal tea ceremony is matcha, a finely ground green tea powder, which is whisked with hot water in a bowl. It takes years to learn how to properly prepare and serve matcha for tea ceremony because of the many ritualistic gestures that accompany it. My grandmother taught tea ceremony from her home for over fifty years,

and even at ninety years of age, she still believed she had much to learn. I gave up trying myself, but I do enjoy drinking matcha in a much more casual way. I just add the powder to a bowl of hot, but not boiling, water and whisk it quickly with a tea whisk called a *chasen*. Matcha has an appealing bitterness, which I love.

There are more than a dozen types of tea in Japan. My choice depends on the weather, the food my tea will accompany, and my mood. For instance, after meals, I often have hojicha, a roasted green tea with a slightly nutty aroma. Sencha, another type of green tea, is made of steamed young leaves. The new crop of sencha comes to market every May, and TV reports track its progress. It's the Beaujolais nouveau of tea. Sencha has a slightly bitter taste, which makes it a good match for *wagashi*, or Japanese sweets.

right: Before making hojicha, I roast it quickly in a dry pan to release more of its aroma.

Wagashi are not like Western treats. They are made of sweet bean paste and sugar but don't contain butter or any other dairy products. They are made to be eaten with tea, and the shapes, colors, and flavors change with the seasons. Like many foods in Japan, the main ingredients and the shapes of wagashi vary by region and season. Some are simple, others quite elaborate and delicately shaped.

When making tea, I usually use an iron tea pot to boil the water. The iron helps neutralize any chlorine taste in the tap water and just seems to make it taste better. It also keeps the water hot longer.

left: An assortment of springtime wagashi, each with a beautiful name: *hanagoromo*, spring clothes; *yuzu manju*, yuzu orange dumpling; *nobe no haru*, dew on the grass; *hanami dango*, flower viewing dumpling.

top: Hojicha, roasted green tea; *genmaicha*, brown rice tea; sencha, whole leaf green tea.

bottom: Sencha served with a special wagashi called hanagoromo.

above: I put scoops of tea into a mesh strainer fitted inside an iron teapot, and let the tea steep for a few minutes. The iron helps neutralize chlorine taste in the tap water and keeps the water hot longer.

above top: Tools for matcha: *chasen*, whisk; *natsume*, jar; *chashaku*, tea scoop.

above bottom: Tea bowl made by Kanako Yamazaki.

above: Making a matcha latte with brewed matcha, milk, sugar, and ice.

Ohanami

The Tradition of Flower Viewing

The days during the cherry blossom season in Tokyo are often still quite chilly. But the billowy pink trees are like a magnet, and my friends and I can't resist taking our meals outdoors and eating underneath their branches. On weekend evenings, we might bring a few snacks and eat those along with sake or tea under the cherry trees. But on the weekends, I like to plan something a bit more elaborate. I'll invite friends for a picnic, even bringing a portable heater and stove, to have the best of both worlds: a little added warmth while eating alfresco. We'll set up a small table and cook *oden*, a type of soup, and friends will bring bento boxes with rice balls; rolled egg omelets, called *tamagoyaki;* fried chicken, or *karaage;* and seasoned rice stuffed into pouches of fried tofu, known as *inarizushi.*

This tradition of *ohanami*, or cherry blossom viewing, started in the eighth century, during the Nara period. At that time, it was plum trees, not cherry trees, that were the object of this adoration. By the Heian period, the practice had fully taken hold and ohanami was synonymous with cherry blossom viewing. But at the time, only those in the Imperial Court participated. Coming at the beginning of spring, ohanami coincided with the annual rice planting. So cherry blossom viewing in those days was decidedly agricultural in focus and centered around making offerings to the gods who inhabited the trees, thereby securing an abundant harvest. Ohanami didn't begin to look like the festival it is today until the seventeenth century, when it began to include the general public and became more of a celebration of spring.

Whether you're surrounded by cherry trees in bloom or not, there's nothing better than a springtime picnic. Being out in the fresh air, hopefully warmed by the sun, and enjoying new growth and an end to winter is invigorating.

Pickled Cherry Blossoms

A Festive Pink Preserve

I make these beautiful pink pickles every spring, as soon as the cherry trees have blossomed. Pickled cherry blossoms (and their leaves) are one of the most traditional preserved foods in Japan. They used to be reserved for celebrations, but now they are used any time we want to experience the delicate flavor of the cherry flower. I add them as an accent to tea or rice, or eat them with sweets. Sometimes, I'll just add them to hot water and enjoy them that way. Their color, harmonious shape, and subtle flavor always makes me happy.

There are different varieties of cherry flowers. The ones used for pickling are called *yamazakura*. They grow all over Japan, but are most often found in the mountains. Their petals are dark pink and tightly layered. When you are picking cherry blossoms, look for new buds that are still partially closed and tender young leaves.

These pickles last for about a year, so you'll be ready to do it all over again when the trees bloom next spring.

MAKES ABOUT ½ CUP [75 G] PICKLES

Several large handfuls (about 4 cups [200 g]) yamazakura cherry blossoms just starting to open, with their leaves, but woody ends removed (make sure these are pesticide free)

⅓ cup plus 2 Tbsp [100 ml] white vinegar

2½ Tbsp kosher salt, plus more for storing the blossoms

Pick through the cherry blossoms, separating the flowers from the leaves and discarding any debris. Wash the blossoms with plenty of water and drain in a colander. Lay the clean blossoms in between sheets of paper towels and press lightly to blot all the excess water. Carefully wash the leaves and blot them dry.

Transfer the blossoms and leaves to a clean glass jar, a widemouthed 1 pt [480 ml] mason jar works well, and add the vinegar and salt. Press a clean, heavy object, such as a large rock, on top of the solids to weigh them down. Let the mixture sit overnight at room temperature.

The next day, pour the contents into a colander and drain for 18 to 24 hours out of direct sunlight. The pickled cherry blossoms are now ready to use. Transfer to a clean jar with a tight-fitting lid, layering the blossoms and leaves with plenty of kosher salt.

Store the pickled blossom in the refrigerator for up to 1 year. Rinse them in water before using.

Resources

USA

Shop Fog Linen
www.shop-foglinen.com
Fog Linen Work online store

Sherry Olsen
www.sherryolsen.com
Artist (I love her ceramics)

JAPAN

Fog Linen Work
www.foglinenwork.com
Linen, clothing, and housewares

The Japan Folk Crafts Museum
www.mingeikan.or.jp
Beautiful collection of crafts and a gift shop

Michinoku Akanekai
www.michinoku-akanekai.com
Homespun woolen scarves

Nobilis Sachiko Shirakawa
+81-3-5701-3022
Florist; delivery only

Ryuji Mitani/+10cm
www.mitaniryuji.com
Beautiful woodcraft

Someya Suzuki
https://someyasuzuki.com
Natural dyed cloth

Tanekara Shoten
www.instagram.com/takita_tanekara/
Organic vegetables

Wataru Ohashi Architect
http://wataruohashi.com
Design house, office building

EUROPE

Fog Linen Europe
https://foglinenworkeurope.com
Fog Linen Work online store

Where to Shop and Eat in Tokyo

SHOPPING

Arts & Science
https://arts-science.com/
Fashion, shoes, bags, art, café

Bingoya
http://bingoya.tokyo
Crafts and folk art

Check and Stripe
http://checkandstripe.com/shop/shop_list
_kichijoji.html
Cute fabric for sewing projects

Cinq
www.cinq-design.com
Good selection of Japanese and Scandinavian housewares

Food for Thought
https://foodforthoughtshop.net
Beautifully handcrafted ceramics, glasses, food

Haibara
www.haibara.co.jp
Japanese traditional paper and stationery

Kanaya Burasi
www.kanaya-brush.com
Specialize in brushes, good for souvenirs

Marks and Web
www.marksandweb.com
Good-quality bath products

Outbound
http://outbound.to
Beautiful housewares, crafts

Saml Waltz and Cinq
http://samlwaltz.com
Treasure hunting, antique furniture

Spiral
www.spiral.co.jp
With a beautiful Japanese tearoom and cute café by Mina Perhonen

Zakka
http://www2.ttcn.ne.jp/zakka-tky.com/index
.html
Hand crafted pottery, textiles, and little café

EATING

Ametsuchi
www.ame-tsuchi.com
If you like sake, this is the perfect place to go

Daikokuya
www.tempura.co.jp
Tempura and small Japanese dishes

Margo
+81-3-5722-4505
Biodynamic wine, good food, and good company

Nanakusa
http://nana-kusa.net/
Beautiful vegetable dishes

Shinoda Sushi
www.kanda-shinodasushi.co.jp/frame.htm
Sushi restaurant and takeout, opened over one hundred years ago

Sushi Horikawa
www.sushi-horikawa.jp
Sushi and seasonal dishes, friendly owner

Tonki
+81-3-3491-9928
Delicious fried pork

Yakumo Saryo
http://yakumosaryo.jp
Very beautiful restaurant, in the middle of nowhere, but worth it

Where to Shop Outside Japan

USA

+COOP
https://shopcoopla.com

Asher + Rye
https://asherandrye.com/

Auntie Oti
www.auntieoti.com

Cavallini Papers & Co
www.cavallini.com

Collyer's Mansion
https://shopthemansion.com/

Coral & Tusk
https://coralandtusk.com

Erica Tanov
www.ericatanov.com

The Gardener
http://thegardener.com

John Derian
www.johnderian.com

Lotta Jansdotter
www.jansdotter.com

March
https://marchsf.com

More & Co
https://alittlemorelikethis.com

Nalata Nalata
https://nalatanalata.com

Nickey Kehoe
https://nickeykehoe.com

Omoi
https://omoionline.com/

Pod
https://shop-pod.com

Quitokeeto
www.quitokeeto.com

Salt House Mercantile
www.salthousemercantile.com

Shoppe Amber Interiors
https://shoppe.amberinteriordesign.com

Sprout Home
https://sprouthome.com/

Take Heart
www.takeheartshop.com/

CANADA

June Home Supply
www.junehomesupply.com/

cont'd

UK

Baileys
www.baileyshome.com

Mouki Mou
www.moukimou.com

No.56
https://no-56.com

Tea & Kate
http://teaandkate.co.uk

Workshop Living
https://workshopliving.co.uk

FRANCE

Les Choses Simples
https://leschosessimples.co

Le Petit Florilège
https://lepetitflorilege.com

NORWAY

Bolina
https://bolina.no

NETHERLANDS

Dreamboat
https://dreamboat.nu

The Fine Store
https://thefinestore.com

Pantoufle
https://pantoufle-design.nl

DENMARK

A Door
https://adoor.dk

FINLAND

Common
https://common-helsinki.com

NEW ZEALAND

Father Rabbit
https://fatherrabbit.com

AUSTRALIA

Hub Furniture
www.hubfurniture.com.au

Imprint House
www.imprinthouse.net

Mr Kitly
https://mrkitly.com.au

Yöli & Otis
www.yoliandotis.com

222
|
223

Thank-Yous

First, I would like to thank my agent, Michele Crim, who first contacted me and encouraged me to consider writing this book. Michele introduced me to the talented Jenny Wapner. Without the two of you, this book would not have happened. Thank you also to everyone at Chronicle Books.

Huge thanks to Nao Shimizu, who took such beautiful photos and made all of my ideas a reality.

Thank you to the Fog Linen team in Tokyo: Masayoshi Kawashima, Sanae Oda, Mayumi Kuchihiro, Remi Asano, Chihiro Yoshida, Haruna Hiraoka, Toki Kasuya, and Saori Tomioka, to Julie Baine and Michael Russem at shop fog linen, and to Olivia Ganslmayr at Fog Linen Europe for all of their help and ideas. And finally, thank you to my family and Wataru.